T0326994

THE FUKUSHIMA NUCLEAR POWER PLANT DISASTER AND THE FUTURE OF RENEWABLE ENERGY

First published 2018 by Cornell University Press

Printed in the United States of America

ISBN 978-1-5017-2693-4

THE FUKUSHIMA NUCLEAR POWER PLANT DISASTER AND THE FUTURE OF RENEWABLE ENERGY

NAOTO KAN

PRIME MINISTER OF JAPAN (2010–2011)

Mario Einaudi Center for International Studies
Distinguished Speaker Series

March 25, 2017
Cornell University

CORNELL GLOBAL PERSPECTIVES

MARIO EINAUDI
Center *for*
International Studies

CORNELL UNIVERSITY PRESS
Ithaca

Naoto Kan spoke at Cornell University as part of the Mario Einaudi Center for International Studies Distinguished Speaker Series. His public lecture was delivered in Japanese. The text was translated for publication by Brett de Bary.

IT HAS NOW BEEN SIX YEARS since the accident at Japan's Fukushima Daiichi Power Plant. A year and a half after its occurrence, I published the book, *My Nuclear Nightmare: Leading Japan Through the Fukushima Disaster to a Nuclear-Free Future*, based on my experience as Prime Minister of Japan at the time of the accident. The English translation of this book has just been published by Cornell University Press and I am deeply grateful. The book offers an account of the situations I faced at the time of the accident, focusing especially on what I confronted during the week that began on March 11, 2011. I would be very pleased if you find my account of what actually happened during this time instructive.

The Great East Japan Earthquake and tsunami

The Great East Japan Earthquake erupted without any warning at 2:46 in the afternoon of March 11, 2011. At that moment, I was attending a meeting of the Audit Committee in our Diet's [Parliament's] Upper House. No sooner had the committee chair announced the recess of the session than I raced to the Crisis Management Center in the Prime Minister's office complex beside the Diet Building. There, reports about the earthquake and tsunami were pouring in in rapid succession. According to these initial reports, all nuclear power plants in areas where the earthquake had occurred had been shut down successfully.

In nuclear power plants, control rods can be automatically inserted between the fuel rods to halt a nuclear fission chain reaction. However, if earthquake damage makes it impossible to insert these rods, there is no way of halting the reaction and a meltdown will occur.

How the accident at Fukushima Daiichi occurred

Despite initial reassurances, about one hour after the earthquake we received another report which announced that the tsunami that followed the earthquake had disabled not only the electrical generators outside the Fukushima Daiichi plant, but also the diesel-fueled equipment intended for emergency back-up use. This meant there was a total loss of power at the plant.

Soon after, we received further news that the cooling system throughout the plant had shut down. I still remember the chill that ran down my spine when I heard this. I am not a specialist in nuclear energy, but as a university student I majored in applied physics and had gained knowledge of the fundamentals of the field. In a power plant, even when nuclear fission chain reactions have been stopped, the decay of nuclear fuel will continue to create massive amounts of heat for a considerable period. I knew that if the cooling systems were disabled there would be a meltdown.

Dysfunction at the government's Nuclear Emergency Response Headquarters

By Japanese law, in the case of a severe accident in which the cooling systems of a nuclear power plant have been disabled, a Nuclear Emergency Response Headquarters is to be set up with the Prime Minister as its head. The Nuclear and Industrial Safety Agency (NISA) within the Ministry of Economy, Trade, and Industry (METI) oversees this disaster headquarters. The reasoning behind this is that the Prime Minister, as a politician, is generally not a specialist in nuclear energy, so a system is in place for government officials who are experts to offer him support.

Therefore, after the accident occurred I immediately summoned the director-general of NISA to obtain his views on three questions. What was the nature of the situation we were facing? How was it likely to develop? What measures should be taken? As it turned out, his response made no sense to me and I could not grasp the gist of his explanations. When I asked him if he was an expert in nuclear energy, this director-general of the Nuclear and Industrial Safety Agency replied that he was a Tokyo University graduate with a degree in economics!

I was stunned by this answer. Of course, since METI also deals with economic policy, it is not surprising for an official to hold a degree in economics. But how can we make sense of the appointment of an economist to be director-general of an agency charged with responding to nuclear accidents? One can only conclude that the assignment of personnel within METI was based on the assumption that a severe nuclear accident would never occur in Japan. Two days later, government officers with expertise in nuclear energy transferred into NISA from other agencies and came to consult with me. It was only at that point that I was able to receive an informed assessment of the situation.

Worsening impact of the accident

Since many politicians and government officials have had experience in dealing with natural disasters like earthquakes and tsunami, they were able to propose response measures quite rapidly. However, there was not a single person among us who had previously dealt with what is classified as a "severe accident" at a nuclear power plant. I received words of advice from members of the Nuclear Safety Commission as well as from members of NISA. I had requested that the head of the Nuclear Safety Commission himself attend my meetings, but in the early moments, no information had arrived about the actual circumstances of the accident, and not a single person could shed light on what its consequences might be. At this stage, I had no choice but to start to set up an organization within my own office to gather information about the accident. My special advisers and executive secretary were at the heart of these activities.

Implications of the accident grow more severe

Over the course of the week following the accident, its consequences increased in gravity. First, after the emergency generators had been disabled by the initial impact of the tsunami, I received a request from TEPCO [the Tokyo Electric Power Company] to coordinate with them in the dispatch of power supply trucks to the site. Since the earthquake had left many highways impassable, I called on police to help with this task. When, at 10 p.m. on the night of March 11, the day of the earthquake, we finally succeeded in getting power supply trucks to the plant, we rejoiced. Yet before long, we received word that the plugs in the trucks could not be connected to the plant. Although we did not understand the problem, ultimately the power supply trucks were useless, and we could not restore power.

At midnight that same night, word arrived that steam pressure was building up inside the containment vessels [also called "containment buildings," these are lead structures enclosing a nuclear reactor and its fuel rods] in the Number One Reactor, and that it would be necessary to release pressure from the vessels. Since radioactive matter would be released together with the steam, however, there was a possibility of harming area residents.

The Nuclear Emergency Response Headquarters, which would be responsible for evacuating residents in such a situation, had received a request for permission to release the pressure. Let me explain that under ordinary conditions, radioactive material from power plants should never be released into the atmosphere. However, if the containment vessels were to burst because they were unable to withstand the pressure, a very large amount of radioactive material would be released all at once. In the view of the Nuclear Safety Commission, the venting of steam pressure was now necessary in order to prevent the vessels from bursting. On this basis, and in the final hours of the night of March 11, we communicated to TEPCO our understanding that the venting would be carried out.

However, in the following several hours, the venting did not take place. Knowing that the chances of the containment vessels bursting were increasing with the delay, I asked the liaison officials from TEPCO headquarters (who had been sent to my offices) why the delay was taking place. The TEPCO officials told me they simply did not know. In other words, I realized at this moment that TEPCO headquarters itself did not have a precise grasp of the situation. It was then that I felt that I would need to speak directly to responsible people at the site of the disaster.

To clarify, TEPCO was responsible for managing the power plant where the accident had occurred. But I, as Prime Minister and head of the Nuclear Emergency Response Headquarters, bore responsibility for the evacuation of residents. I went to Fukushima because I felt that I would need to have an accurate knowledge of the situation at the power plant in order to determine the radius of evacuation.

On the morning after the accident, I went by helicopter to talk directly with the responsible parties at the site. Although I was criticized by the media and the opposition parties for hastiness in absenting myself from the Prime Minister's office complex, I felt it was important to get an accurate view of what had happened. At the site, I was able to meet the plant manager, Masao Yoshida, and to speak with him. Mr. Yoshida was a straightforward man who made a favorable impression on me. His explanation of the situation was very clear: "Under ordinary circumstances the venting system is operated by a switch, but because the electrical power in the plant is out, this will have to be done manually. This is a risky job, because radiation levels near the valve that would need to be manipulated are very high. But, do or die, we'll get the job done."

I wished him good luck as I left the plant. I felt Mr. Yoshida was someone I could trust.

Worst-case scenario

The first week after the accident was a nightmare. More accidents occurred one after another. Although we only learned this from investigations later, by 6 p.m. on March 11, the first day of the accident, a meltdown had occurred at the Unit 1 reactor. This was only three hours after the initial earthquake. At 10 p.m. that night, we received reports from the site that water had overflowed the spent fuel rods. This was because no one had realized that the water gauge was malfunctioning.

On the following day, March 12, a hydrogen explosion occurred at the Unit 1 reactor. Another occurred at the Unit 3 reactor on March 14. On March 15, when I was at TEPCO headquarters, sounds of an explosion came from the Unit 2 reactor, and almost simultaneously there was a hydrogen explosion at the Unit 4 reactor.

When the accident first occurred, the United States government issued a directive requiring American citizens within a 50-mile (80-kilometer) radius of the Fukushima power plant to leave. Many European embassies in Tokyo closed down, and their personnel began to be moved to the Kansai area.

If all the reactors at the Fukushima power plant were to become dysfunctional, the entire plant, together with the cooling pools that contain spent fuel, would melt down in a matter of a few weeks or months, and massive amounts of radioactive material would be released. I understood that if this were to happen, an evacuation of all the people within a large area, including the city of Tokyo, would be unavoidable.

On March 22, about ten days after the earthquake, when cooling by water pumps had begun and I was feeling we had narrowly escaped the worst, I had my special advisor, Mr. Gōshi Hosono, convey a message to Dr. Shunsuke Kondō, the chair of the Japan Atomic Energy Commission. I requested that the commission conduct a scientific evaluation of the area that would have to be evacuated in the event of multiple "worst-case scenarios." This scientific study is what the media have referred to as "the Prime Minister's office's worst-case scenario." It came in the form of a document delivered to me on March 25 from Dr. Kondō entitled "Rough Sketch of a Contingency Plan for the Fukushima Daiichi Power Plant."

Dr. Kondō's was a highly technical document. It stated that, "If Unit 1's containment vessel is destroyed by a hydrogen explosion, increased radiation levels would force the plant's workers to evacuate the site. It would then be impossible to and cool Units 2 and 3 with water. Radioactive material will be discharged by these reactors and by the spent fuel pools in Units 1 through 4, and there is the possibility that a forced evacuation would be required for an area within a 170-kilometer (106-mile) radius of the site and a voluntary evacuation area of 250 kilometers (155 miles), including Tokyo." Here was scientific confirmation, from a specialist, of my own worst nightmare! As I read it, a chill went down my spine.

The 250-mile radius around Fukushima included a large part of the Kantō region, containing the city of Tokyo; the population of this radius is about 50 million people. An evacuation on that scale would be necessary. Dr. Kondō also calculated that, based on the amount of time necessary for radioactive material to decay on its own, it would take several decades before the evacuated areas were suitable for human habitation again. The evacuation of 50 million people from their homes for a period of several decades would have been an event without precedent in any country in the world!

While the stoicism with which the Japanese responded to the events of March 11 won admiration around the world, an evacuation of 50 million people would be a veritable hell. It would mean the upending of 50 million lives. Unlike moving to a new residence, evacuees flee leaving their belongings behind. What can they carry with them? Can they move as a family? Where will they go? And if they find a place to go, will they find jobs? Unimaginable hardship and confusion would ensue. Yet there was nothing "imaginary" about this forecast. We were a hair's breadth away from this actuality.

The anguish of bearing ultimate responsibility

For one week following March 11, 2011, eastern Japan was on the verge of being occupied by an enemy: radiation. This enemy was not an invader from outside. While many Japanese did not think of it this way, this was an enemy the Japanese people had created for themselves. This was all the more reason they should bring the situation under control.

In order to cope with the Chernobyl crisis [in 1986 in present-day Ukraine], the Soviet Union mobilized its army to extinguish fires by dropping 5,000 tons of sand and lead onto them from helicopters. Within a half a year of the disaster, the "stone sarcophagus" was constructed. It was reported that about 30 people, mainly firefighters, died from intense exposure to radiation during just the first ten days of working to extinguish fires. I have heard that military personnel, who were the next to be mobilized, also died in considerable numbers. However, if we were to do nothing about the reactors just because the work of dealing with them was dangerous, the risk of having even greater numbers of victims would be very high.

Faced with the actuality of the nuclear accident that had occurred at Fukushima Daiichi, I had no one but myself to turn to in thinking about these issues. Knowing that in the worst-case scenario people might die, could I ask them to go to the plant to help? I resolved that it was I, as Prime Minister, who would have to make this excruciating judgment. As I will describe, it was when I arrived at the TEPCO headquarters shortly after 5 a.m. on March 15, 2011, that this dire question confronted me in all its reality.

TEPCO's retreat and the consolidated headquarters

At 3 o'clock in the morning of March 15, as I was taking a short nap in the Prime Minister's offices, my executive secretary awakened me to announce the arrival of the Minister of Economy, Trade, and Industry, Mr. Banri Kaieda. He told me that he had been informed by TEPCO's president, Masataka Shimizu, that TEPCO wished to allow its employees to leave Fukushima Daiichi.

One cannot fault Mr. Shimizu, as president of TEPCO, for wanting to allow his employees to leave a plant that had become highly dangerous. Yet, I had to ask what would become of the plant if these employees left. Key TEPCO personnel who knew how to operate the plant could not be replaced. Abandoning the reactors would mean that the situation would worsen in a matter of hours. Fuel would not be consumed, a meltdown would take place, and radioactive materials would start to be released into the environment. The increased damage resulting from this was incalculable.

The discussions over whether or not TEPCO would abandon the site continued through the night of the 14th until dawn on March 15. The import of that possibility was clear, however. If the ten reactors and 11 spent fuel pools were abandoned, Japan itself would be decimated.

My view was that to abandon the site was unthinkable. This view extended not only to TEPCO, but also to the Japan Self-Defense Force, the fire department, and the police. In ordinary circumstances, this would be asking too much from a private corporation. But TEPCO was the party responsible for the accident, and the nuclear reactor at the Fukushima plant could only be operated by TEPCO technicians. Without them, there was simply no way to bring the situation under control. For these reasons, I could not allow TEPCO to withdraw, even if it meant putting lives at risk.

In order to get TEPCO to join forces with the government, I concluded that it would be necessary to set up a joint command center staffed by both, and located at the TEPCO headquarters. And yet even on the grave question of TEPCO's requested withdrawal, we did not have smooth communication. Communication problems could very well be fatal to the process of trying to come up with a strategy for containing the disaster. I therefore called Mr. Shimizu to my offices. "TEPCO's withdrawal is not an option," I told him. I proposed that we set up an Integrated Response Center in TEPCO's offices, and he agreed.

In order to launch the Integrated Response Center, I went to TEPCO's headquarters at 5:30 in the morning on March 15. Since I assumed that the plan to withdraw from the plant reflected the view, not only of President Shimizu, but also of the CEO and other executives, it was my intention personally to try to persuade them to drop the plan. Summoning all the strength I could muster, I addressed them as follows:

More than anyone, you know the gravity of the situation we are in. There is a need for the government and TEPCO to strategize together, in real time. I will be the director, and Minister Kaieda and President Shimizu will be the deputy directors. I'm not just concerned about Unit 2. If we abandon Unit 2, what will happen to 1, 3, 4, 5, and 6? And what will happen to the Fukushima Daini plant [a sister plant about ten kilometers (six miles) to the south]?

If we withdraw, within months all the reactors and nuclear waste will further deteriorate, resulting in the spread of radiation. It would be two or three times the size of Chernobyl, equal to ten or 20 reactors.

Japan will cease to exist if we don't risk our lives to bring this situation under control. We cannot withdraw quietly and watch from afar. If we were to do that, it would not be out of the question for a foreign country to come along and take our place.

You are all party to this, so I ask you to put your lives on the line. There is nowhere to run. Communication is slow, inaccurate, and often mistaken. Don't become dispirited. Provide the information that is needed. Take in what is happening now, but also look five hours, ten hours, a day, a week ahead, and act accordingly. It doesn't matter how much it costs.

No one can do this but TEPCO. When Japan is at risk of failure, withdrawal is out of the question. Mr. Chairman and Mr. President, prepare yourselves. Employees who are over 60 should go to the site. I, too, will work with this resolve. Withdrawal is out of the question. If you withdraw, TEPCO will inevitably fail.

I am repeating this speech for you based on notes taken by one of my staff members who attended the meeting.

Damage to the Unit 2 reactor

At 6 o'clock in the morning of March 15, shortly after I had visited TEP-CO headquarters to urge them not to withdraw, but to do everything in their power to bring the situation under control, I received a report from the Onsite Response Headquarters in Fukushima. Sounds of a blast were coming from some place near the Unit 2 reactor's suppression chamber. At the same time, the internal pressure in the containment buildings had reached the same level as the external pressure [which could lead to an explosion]. A hole was visible in one part of the suppression chamber.

Later investigations revealed that the source of the greatest radioactive emissions during this period had been the Unit 2 reactor. Had the unit's entire containment vessel been destroyed at that time, the possibility that my worst-case scenario would unfold was very high. It was, in fact, precisely because pressure in the Unit 2 containment building had dropped that we were able to pump water into the reactor.

Counterattack

Once the Integrated Response Center had been established at TEPCO's headquarters, communications between TEPCO and the government gradually grew more efficient. In the case of draining water from the spent fuel-rod pools, for example, we were able greatly to improve the system for cooperation between the Self-Defense Force and the police.

It was on March 16, the day after the Integrated Response Center was set up, that the Self-Defense Force was able to use helicopters to bring in water to be pumped into the spent fuel-rod pools, the first move forward in a counter-attack against the relentless assault of radioactivity released by the accidents. Because a high level of radioactivity was being emitted into the atmosphere above the plant that day, on March 17 we brought in water by helicopter and commenced a life-or-death battle to get water into the plants. It was at this juncture that a wave of determination swept across the ranks of the Self-Defense Force, firefighters, and police to save Japan at the risk of their own lives.

Moreover, a reduction of pressure in the Unit 1, 2, and 3 containment vessels had made the pumping in of water possible. As a result, it became possible to cool the nuclear fuel and gradually to reduce the heat it produced, stabilizing each of the reactors.

By the grace of the gods

As I have said, if venting the Unit 2 reactor had been delayed and pressure had risen within its containment vessel, explosions would have erupted that shattered the entire reactor like a balloon and we would have confronted my worst-case scenario. We escaped this only because the containment vessel was not destroyed, but survived with partial damage.

It was due to the heroic efforts of the TEPCO employees, the Self-Defense Force members, firefighters, and police, that we escaped the worst-case scenario. However, it was not for this reason alone. I cannot help feeling that we escaped, as they say, "by the grace of the gods."

Several lucky accidents came into play. One was that the Unit 4 reactor happened to have water in its spent fuel rod pool. Because of a delay in construction work, the upper part of this reactor happened to have been filled with water on the day of the accident. It is thought that the wooden partition between the upper level and the pool below warped that day, allowing water from the one into the other. Had there been no water flowing into the pool at the time, the spent fuel rods that were being transferred into the pool would have undergone meltdown, and there would have been no way to avert the worst-case scenario.

Thanks to this good fortune, we escaped the worst, and I never had to confront a situation that required formulating a concrete evacuation plan. The "50 million person evacuation simulation" that had been constantly playing itself out in my mind came to a stop. Nevertheless, that worst-case scenario occupies a part of my mind to this very day.

The cause of the accident

Why did the accident happen? The direct cause was the impact of the March 11 earthquake and tsunami that caused a total loss of power at the Fukushima Daiichi Nuclear Power Plant. Nevertheless, Japan is a country that has experienced numerous earthquakes, and been inundated by tsunami any number of times.

The accident occurred because the plant was built without paying adequate attention to these factors.

The Fukushima plant was designed to be built on a bluff overlooking the Pacific Ocean, 35 meters above sea level. However, when the reactors were constructed, earth was removed from the bluff to bring it down to an elevation of 10 meters above sea level. Had the reactors been located at 35 meters above sea level, the tsunami would not have reached them and the accident would not have occurred. The elevation was lowered to reduce the cost of electricity needed to pump in water from the ocean for cooling purposes.

It is also said that, several years before the accident, researchers at TEPCO had noted the possibility of a 17-meter tsunami hitting the plant. But TEPCO courted disaster by never formulating a contingency plan. At the present time, responsibility for the accident is being adjudicated in court.

Reviewing our basic energy plan

Prior to the Fukushima accident, Japan had provided for 30 percent of its energy needs through nuclear energy, and had planned to increase this to 50 percent by 2030. After the accident, I called for a review of the Basic Energy Plan that had recommended this increase, with the aim of reversing Japan's course in the direction of nuclear-free energy. Furthermore, I requested that Chūbu Electric halt operation of the Hamaoka Power Plant, which was located above an earthquake hypocenter, at the junction of two tectonic plates. My request was granted.

To help replace nuclear energy, I also introduced a system developed in Germany 20 years ago for establishing fixed prices for the purchase of energy generated from renewable sources, which would make it possible to expand the use of renewable energy. When I resigned as Prime Minister in September 2011, and was replaced by Prime Minister [Yoshihiko] Noda (a member, like me, of the Democratic Party of Japan), we resolved to reduce Japan's dependence on nuclear energy to zero by 2030.

However, the Democratic Party regrettably suffered a major defeat in the 2012 elections, while the LDP [Liberal Party of Japan] saw a resurgence of political power. The LDP decided to maintain a nuclear energy supply of 20 to 22 percent. Today, they are gradually restoring 44 reactors to operation. However, the Japanese population at large is against this policy, and in a number of cases courts have stopped orders to restart the plants. For this reason, only three nuclear power plants are operational in Japan today.

The situation at Fukushima today

The situation at the Fukushima power plant has still not yet been brought under control. More than 100,000 people still live as evacuees. Among the reactors at the plant, Units 1, 2, and 3, have had meltdowns, and water is still being pumped in to cool the nuclear debris. Some of this water, having been contaminated by radiation, has been leaking out from the containment vessels.

Following the example of Three Mile Island [a U.S. nuclear power plant that suffered a partial meltdown in 1979], TEPCO and METI have come up with a plan to complete the collection and incineration of the radioactive debris over about a 40-year period. However, I doubt whether this plan is feasible. Even at Three Mile Island, where the reactor's pressure vessels were left intact, debris had accumulated in the vessels. It was for this reason that a submersion method was used at Three Mile Island— that is, the pressure vessels were filled with water—to block the emission of radiation, allowing the debris to be extracted.

In the case of Units 1, 2, and 3 at Fukushima, however, the pressure vessels have been melted by heat and have holes in them. This caused debris to be scattered throughout the containment vessels. The radiation levels are so high inside that even one minute of exposure is lethal. To deal with the debris would require flooding the entire containment vessel, but the holes make this much more difficult to do than it had been at Three Mile Island.

At Chernobyl, a giant metal dome has been placed over the No. 4 reactor because, even after the passage of 30 years, radiation continues to leak from the stone sarcophagus. But there is still no plan at all for removing debris in Chernobyl. My guess is that the process at Fukushima will take more than 100 years.

Energy conservation and renewable energy

As a result of the Fukushima accident, interest in matters related to energy has been heightened in Japan, and the situation surrounding energy use continues to change. Energy consumption in general in Japan now is down by 10 percent from its 2010 levels, prior to the Fukushima accident. People have a greater awareness of the importance of conserving energy, and this has resulted in measures undertaken at workplaces, large buildings, and private residences to reduce energy use.

In private homes, for example, it is becoming more common for people to install two or three layers of glass in their windows to conserve heat, and the number of households that have reduced their heating expenses to zero by installing solar panels on rooftops is growing. In 2013, I had my own home converted to an energy-saving home. By installing a 5-kilowatt solar panel on the roof, I now have a negative balance on my energy bills, and my heating bills are zero.

The introduction of FIT and expansion of renewable energy

Although many countries had increased their use of wind and solar energy before the Fukushima accident, in Japan at the time water-generated electrical energy accounted for only 10 percent of electrical energy used, and the use of other renewable sources of energy had not been promoted at all. This was because the vested interests in nuclear energy have had a great deal of power, and were able to suppress the development of renewable energy sources.

I came to believe in the necessity of encouraging the use of renewable sources—solar power, wind power, biomass—as a means of ending our reliance on nuclear power and fossil fuels.

Thus, three months after Fukushima, I took as my last task as Prime Minister the job of proposing to the Diet a bill for the establishment of a FIT ["feed-in-tariff"] system in Japan. [A FIT allows consumers generating renewable energy to be paid for feeding energy back into the power grid.] Since the introduction of the FIT system, the use of renewable energy, and especially solar power, has grown in Japan. By 2015, solar energy generators in every prefecture were producing an amount of energy equal to that of five nuclear reactors. We expect that by 2020, this will exceed the production of ten nuclear reactors.

Combining agriculture and forestry with renewable energy generation

In recent years, the possibility of combining farming with solar energy production has attracted attention in Japan. The country's plains are dotted with wide swaths of rice paddies. Yet the population in rural areas has declined, because rice prices have fallen and farming the paddies no longer generates sufficient income. In the past few years, however, methods have been developed for cultivating rice and vegetables while generating solar power, and these are attracting interest. For example, by implementing a practice called "solar sharing," farmers can install posts about three meters high in rice paddies and vegetable gardens, and use them to support solar panels at regular intervals. In this way, sunlight can be "shared" between crops and the panels. If this practice spreads in Japan, which has 4,600,000 hectares of agricultural land, the country could supply over half of its energy from farmland.

Nuclear reactors in other countries

In concluding my talk, I would like to introduce a few thoughts about nuclear power in countries I have been invited to visit.

Within a few months of the Fukushima accident, Germany decided to close down all of its nuclear plants by 2020. In truth, I think Japan should be the first nation to reduce its use of nuclear energy to zero, but regrettably, it appears that this will not happen.

The first group to invite me to visit after the events of Fukushima was a citizens' group in California opposing restarting the San Onofre Nuclear Generating Station. I participated in a symposium there with Gregory

Jaczko, who had been serving as the chair of the U.S. Nuclear Regulatory Commission at the time of the Fukushima accident. A few days later, Southern California Edison, owners of the plant, decided to decommission it. In the United States, nuclear power plants tend to be fewer on the West Coast, which is prone to earthquakes, and more numerous on the East Coast. Yet even in America, closings of nuclear power plants are outnumbering the construction of new ones, leaving a total of 100 reactors in operation.

Following my visit to California, I was invited by anti-nuclear groups to visit Korea, Poland, the UK, and Taiwan. Taiwan decommissioned its newly constructed No. 4 reactor, and has resolved to move to zero reliance on nuclear power by 2025. Even in France, which matches the United States in the scale of its development of nuclear energy, Prime Minister Hollande publicly vowed to reduce the proportion of energy supplied by nuclear power plants from 75 percent to 50 percent, and cut back on the construction of new plants.

A chief reason for this reduction is that costs have risen, pushing the price of electricity generated by nuclear power plants above that generated from renewable sources. Nuclear energy has become less profitable. In England, for example, the government has approved the closing down of older nuclear power plants and approved the building of new ones. But it has proven difficult to raise funds from the private sector to support the new construction, so companies are turning to the government for assistance.

Energy independence for all nations

Scientists have calculated that the amount of energy radiated from the sun to the earth is 10,000 times greater than the energy used by the earth's human population. By this logic, if humans could effectively harness even one-thousandth of that power, it would be sufficient to satisfy their needs for electricity and heat. If we made use of the technologies available to us today, almost every nation in the world would be able to produce enough energy from renewable sources like wind and solar power to satisfy its energy needs.

If every nation in the world could satisfy its own energy needs, struggles for resources among nations—like the global competition for oil—would no longer arise.

The use of renewable, natural energy, and the end of reliance on nuclear energy and fossil fuels, can open a path to a peaceful world. It is my intention to commit myself without respite toward the achievement of this goal.

ABOUT NAOTO KAN

Naoto Kan (born October 10, 1946) was prime minister of Japan from June 2010 to September 2011. He has also served as deputy prime minister, finance minister, health minister, and national strategy minister.

The son of a corporate employee in the southern prefecture of Yamaguchi, Kan graduated with a degree in physics from the Tokyo Institute of Technology, where he was involved the student movement, then worked for a patent firm.

In 1980, after three unsuccessful attempts, he won a seat in parliament as part of the tiny Social Democratic Federation. He served as health minister under a coalition deal with the Liberal Democratic Party (LDP) in the mid-1990s, becoming widely known after he exposed a scandal involving HIV-contaminated blood products.

He played a leading role in the formation of the Democratic Party of Japan (DPJ), which helped sweep the LDP from power in September 2009. Kan became prime minister after the resignation of fellow Democratic Party member Yukio Hatoyama in 2010. He inherited a divided parliament, a stagnating economy, and massive public debt. He resigned less than six months after the Fukushima disaster.

ABOUT THE EINAUDI CENTER

The Mario Einaudi Center for International Studies was established in 1961 to enhance Cornell's research and teaching about the world's regions, countries, cultures, and languages. In 1990 it was named for its founding director, the political theorist Mario Einaudi. Today the center houses area studies and thematic programs; organizes speaker series, conferences, and events; provides grants and support to faculty and students; and brings together scholars from many disciplines to address complex international issues.

福島原発事故と再生可能エネルギーの将来

菅　直人

第94代内閣総理大臣

マリオ・エイナウディ国際学センター特別栄誉講演

2017年3月25日コーネル大学

はじめに

福島原発事故発生から6年が経過しました。事故発生の1年半後に出版した私の著書「福島原発事故、総理大臣として考えたこと」の英訳本を今回コーネル大学出版会が出版してくださることになり、心から感謝しています。この本は福島原発事故に直面した2011年3月11日からの1週間を中心に、私自身が直面した事実をまとめたものです。福島原発事故の真実の姿を知るうえで参考にしてくだされば幸いです。

東日本大震災の発生

2011年3月11日、午後2時46分、東日本大震災は突然発生しました。その時私は、参院の決算委員会に出席していました。委員長が休憩を宣言した後すぐに、国会の隣にある官邸の危機管理センターに駆け込みました。そして地震、津波に関する報告を次々と受けました。原発に関する最初の報告は地震が発生した地域にある原発はすべて無事に停止したというものでした。ほっとしたのを覚えています。原発は燃料棒の間に制御棒を挿入して核分裂反応を止めることになっていますが、もし地震で原発が壊れて制御棒が挿入できなくなっていれば、核分裂反応が止まず、大事故につながるからです。

原発事故の発生

しかし地震発生から約1時間後に来た次の報告は、地震に続く津波により、外部電源だけでなく緊急用のディーゼル発電機もダウンし、福島第一原発の全ての電源が喪失したというものでした。さらに続いて、原発の全ての冷却機能が停止したという報告が届きました。私はこの報告が来た時に背筋がぞっとしたのを今でも思い出します。私は原子力の専門家ではありませんが、大学では応用物理科に席を置いていたので、原子力について基本的なことは学んでいまし

た。原発では核分裂反応を停止させても、自己崩壊熱という膨大な熱が相当期間発生し続けるため、冷却機能が停止すればメルトダウンが起こることを知っていたからです。

機能しない原災本部事務局

冷却機能が停止するような原発のシビア・アクシデントが発生した時に、日本の法律では総理大臣を本部長とする原災本部を設置することになっていました。そして原災本部の事務局は経産省の原子力安全・保安院が担うことになっています。大臣となる政治家は一般的には原子力の専門家ではありませんから、原子力の専門家である官僚が大臣をサポートする体制に当然なっているだろうと考えていました。そこで私は、事故発生後まず、原子力安全・保安院のトップを呼んで、①現状はどうなっているか。②これからどうなりそうか。③どういう対策を打てばよいか、という３点について意見を求めました。しかし、院長の説明は要領を得ず、私には理解できませんでした。そこで私が「あなたは原子力の専門家ですか」と尋ねると原子力安全・保安院の院長は「私は東大の経済学部出身です」と答えました。

　これには驚きました。もちろん、経産省は経済官庁でもあるので、経済学部出身者がいるのは当然です。しかし、原発事故が起きた時にその対応に当たる原子力安全・保安院のトップが原子力の専門家でないというのは一体どういうことでしょうか。つまり原発のシビア・アクシデントは絶対に起きないことを前提とした経産省の人事配置であったということです。２日後になって、経産省のほかの部門にいた原子力に詳しい官僚が原子力安全・保安院に移籍して、私のところにやってきました。その段階でようやくまともな状況説明を聞くことができるようになりました。

原発事故の深刻化

地震や津波災害といった自然災害については、政治家にも官僚にも経験したことのあるメンバーが多くいたので、迅速に対策を打ち出すことができました。しかし、原発のシビア・アクシデントを経験

したことのある人は誰一人いませんでした。原発事故に当たっては原子力安全・保安院に加えて、原子力の専門家からなる原子力安全委員会が助言を行うことになっていました。原子力安全委員会からも委員長に来てもらいましたが、当初は福島原発事故の現場の情報が届いておらず、原発事故が今後どのような展開を示すのか誰にも予想がつきませんでした。私はやむなく、事故発生後の早い段階から、総理補佐官や総理秘書官を中心に、官邸に原発事故の情報収集のための体制を作り始めました。

事故の深刻化

原発事故発生から1週間、事故はどんどん深刻化していきました。緊急用発電機が津波をかぶって停止したのち、東電から電源車を送りたいので協力してほしいという要請が来ました。地震の影響で多くの道路が通行止めになっていたので、私はすぐに警察に支援するよう指示しました。そして3月11日の午後10時ごろようやく最初の電源車が現場に到着し、これで大丈夫だと喜びました。しかし、しばらくして電源車と原発の接続ができないという報告が届きました。電力会社でありながら、接続ができないのはどういうことか理解できませんでしたが、結局、送られた電源車は役に立たず、電源は回復しませんでした。

　また11日の深夜になって東電から1号機で格納容器の圧力が上がってきたために格納容器内の水蒸気を外に出すベントを行いたいと言ってきました。ベントをすれば放射性物質も外に出るので、住民に被害が及ぶ可能性があります。そのために住民避難について責任を負っている原災本部に了解を求めて来たのです。通常は放射性物質を外に出すベントはやりません。しかし格納容器が圧力に耐えられず破壊すれば大量の放射性物質が一挙に放出されます。そうした事態を防ぐためにはベントを行うこともやむを得ないというのが、原子力安全委員会の意見でした。そこで11日の深夜、東電に対しベントの実施を了解すると伝えました。

　しかし了解してから数時間経過してもベントが行われません。ベントが遅れれば格納容器が破壊する可能性があると聞かされていたので、なぜベントを行わないのかと東電本店から連絡要員として官邸に

来ていた東電の役員に尋ねました。それに対して東電の役員は「分かりません」と答えました。つまり、東電本店は現場の状況をきちんとは把握できていないのだと分かりました。私はこの時、事故現場の責任者と直接話す必要があると考えました。

　つまり、事故を起こした原発をどう操作するかという責任は東電にあります。しかし、原発周辺の住民避難は私が本部長の原子力災害対策本部の責任です。避難の範囲を判断するうえで、原発の状況を正確に知っておく必要があると考えたからです。私は事故発生の翌日の早朝に、現地の責任者と直接話すためにヘリコプターで福島第一原発を訪れました。マスコミや野党から総責任者である総理が官邸を離れるのは軽率だという批判もありましたが、私は原発の状況を正確に知ることの方が重要だと考えたのです。現地では責任者の吉田所長に直接会って、話をしました。吉田所長は物事をはっきり言う人物で、好感が持てました。「通常ならベントはスイッチを押せばできるが、電源がないために人手で作業を行う必要があります。弁を人手で操作する場所の放射線量が高いので作業が難航しています。しかし最終的には決死隊を作ってでも実行します」と明確な説明をしてくれました。私は「頑張ってください」と言い残して福島原発を出発しました。吉田所長は信頼できる男だと感じました。

最悪のシナリオ

原発事故が発生してからの一週間は悪夢でした。事故は次々と拡大していきました。これは後の検証で分かったことですが、事故発生初日の３月１１日午後6時頃、すでに一号機ではメルトダウンが始まっていました。地震発生からわずか3時間半後です。当日の午後10時ごろ水が燃料棒の上まであるという報告が現地から来ていましたが、これは水位計が誤動作しているのが分からなかったからです。翌１２日午後には一号機で水素爆発が起きました。 14日には3号機で水素爆発。そして15日、私が東電本店にいた午前6時頃、2号機で衝撃音があったと報告され、ほぼ同時に4号機で水素爆発が起きました。

　事故発生後、米国は福島原発から50マイル（80キロ）の範囲からの退避を日本にいる米国民に指示していました。多くのヨーロッパ諸国は東京の大使館を閉め、関西への移転を始めていました。

菅　直人

　福島原発の全ての原発が制御不能になれば、数週間から数か月の間に全原発と使用済み核燃料プールがメルトダウンし、膨大な放射性物質が放出されます。そうなれば、東京を含む広範囲の地域からの避難は避けられないと私は考えていました。事故発生から10日ほど後、冷却のための注水作業が始まり、最悪の危機を脱しつつあると思われた２２日頃、細野豪志補佐官を通して、原子力委員会の委員長、近藤駿介氏に、最悪の事態が重なった場合に、どの程度の範囲が避難区域になるかを予測して欲しいと依頼しました。これが「官邸が作っていた『最悪のシナリオ』」とマスコミが呼んでいるもので、３月25日に近藤氏から届いた「福島第一原子力発電所の不測事態シナリオの素描」という文書のことです。

　これは最悪の仮説を置いての極めて技術的な予測であり、「水素爆発で１号機の原子炉格納容器が壊れ、放射線量が上昇して作業員全員が撤退したとの想定で、注水による冷却ができなくなった２号機、３号機の原子炉や、１号機から４号機の使用済み核燃料プールから放射性物質が放出されると、強制移転区域は半径１７０キロ以上、希望者の移転を認める区域が東京都を含む半径２５０キロに及ぶ可能性がある」と書かれていました。

　私が個人的に考えていたことが、専門家によって科学的に裏付けられたことになり、やはりそうであったかと、背筋が凍りつく思いでした。

福島原発から250キロ圏となると、東京を含む関東の大部分が含まれ、この範囲内には約５千万人の日本人が居住しています。つまり、５千万人の避難が必要ということになります。近藤氏の「最悪のシナリオ」では放射線量が人間が暮らせるようになるまでの避難期間は、自然減衰にのみ任せた場合で、数十年を要するとも予測されていました。「５千万人の数十年にわたる避難」となると、過去に参考になる事例など外国にもないでしょう。

　大震災における日本人の冷静な行動は国際的に評価されましたが、五千万人の避難となれば、それこそ地獄絵です。５千万人の人生が破壊されてしまいます。引越しではないので、家財道具はそのままにして逃げることになります。何を持って行けるのか。家族は一緒に行動できるのか。どこへ避難するのか。どうにか避難したとして、仕事はどうする。家はどうする。子どもの学校はどうなる。想像を絶する困難と混乱が待ち受けていたでしょう。そしてこれは空想の話ではない。紙一重で現実となった話なのです。

最高責任者としての悩み

2011年3月11日からの１週間、東日本は放射能という見えない敵によって占領されようとしていました。その敵は、外国からの侵略者ではありません。多くの人にとって、そのような意識はないでしょうが、日本人自身が生み出した敵なのです。であればこそ、日本が自分の力で収束させなければなりませんでした。

　ソ連ではチェルノブイリ原発事故を収束させるために、軍が出動してヘリコプターから総計五千トンの砂や鉛を投下して消火し、さらに半年ほどかけて「石棺」を作りました。最初の１０日ほどの消火作業だけで消防士を中心に、約３０名が急性被曝で死亡したと伝えられています。その後動員された兵士のうち相当数の兵士が死亡したと言われています。しかし危険な作業だからと言って原発を放置すれば、さらに被害が広がった可能性が高いのです。

　実際に起きた福島原発事故を前にして私は一人考えていました。内閣総理大臣である私は、最悪の場合死ぬ恐れがあると知りながら、「行ってくれ」と要請することができるのか。ぎりぎりの判断は総理である私がすることになることを覚悟していました。私が東電本店に乗り込んだ3月15日の午前５時過ぎ、このような切羽詰まった問題が、現実として目の前に迫っていました。

東電撤退と統合本部

3月15日午前３時、私が官邸で仮眠をとっていた時に秘書官から「経産大臣が相談したいことがあると言って来ています」と起こされました。そして海江田万里経産大臣がやって来て、東電の清水正孝社長から福島第一原発から東電関係者を撤退させたいという申し出があったと告げられました。

　東電の社長として、危険性が高くなった福島第一原発から社員を撤退させたいと考えたことは決して非難されることではありません。しかし、東電の社員が撤退したら、原発はどうなるのか。東電関係者に代わって原発をコントロールできる要員はどこにもいません。原子炉が放置されれば、時間の経過とともに事態は悪化していきます。燃料は燃え尽きず、メルトダウンを起こし、放射性物質を

放出し始めます。その結果どこまでも被害が拡大することになることが予想されました。

　事故発生から４日目の１４日夜から１５日未明にかけて、東電が事故現場から撤退するという話が持ち上がりましたが、それが意味するのは、福島第一原発にある１０基の原発と１１の使用済み核燃料プールを放棄することであり、それによって日本が壊滅するかどうかという問題だったのです。

　私は、撤退はあり得ないと考えていました。それは東電だけでなく、自衛隊や消防、警察についても同じ気持ちでした。民間企業である東電社員にそこまで要求するのは通常であれば行き過ぎでしょう。しかし、東電は事故を起こした当事者であり、事故を起こした東電福島原発の原子炉を操作できるのは東電の技術者以外にはいません。事故を収束させることは、東電関係者抜きでは不可能です。それだけに、たとえ生命の危険があろうとも、東電に撤退してもらうわけにはいかないのです。

　私は同時に、東電と政府の意思決定を一元化するため、政府と東電の統合対策本部を東電本店内に設けることが必要と判断しました。事故に対しては東電と政府が一体であたらなくてはならないのに、撤退問題といった重要問題でさえ意思疎通が十分でなかったのです。こうした意思の疎通が悪いことは事故の収束作戦を進める上で、致命傷になりかねないと考えたからです。そこで、清水社長を官邸に呼び、「撤退はない」と言い渡し、また「統合対策本部を東電本店内に置く」ことを提案し、了解を取り付けました。

　私は、統合対策本部を立ち上げるため３月１５日午前５時半ごろ、東電本店に乗り込みました。「撤退」は清水社長だけの考えではなく、会長など他の幹部の判断も当然入っていたと考えたので、私は、会長、社長など東電幹部を前に、撤退を思いとどまるように説得するつもりで、渾身の力を気持ちに込めて次のように話しました。

　「今回の事故の重大性は皆さんが一番分かっていると思う。政府と東電がリアルタイムで対策を打つ必要がある。私が本部長、海江田大臣と清水社長が副本部長ということになった。これは２号機だけの話ではない。２号機を放棄すれば、１号機、３号機、４号機から６号機、さらには福島第二のサイト、これらはどうなってしまうのか。これらを放棄した場合、何か月後かには、すべての原発、核廃棄物が崩壊して放射能を発することになる。チェル

ノブイリの二倍から三倍のものが１０基、２０基と合わさる。日本の国が成立しなくなる。

　何としても、命懸けで、この状況を抑え込まない限りは、撤退して黙って見過ごすことはできない。そんなことをすれば、外国が『自分たちがやる』と言い出しかねない。皆さんは当事者です。命を懸けてください。逃げても逃げ切れない。情報伝達は遅いし、不正確だ。しかも間違っている。皆さん、萎縮しないでくれ。必要な情報を上げてくれ。目の前のこととともに、１０時間先、１日先、１週間先を読み、行動することが大切だ。

　金がいくらかかっても構わない。東電がやるしかない。日本がつぶれるかもしれない時に撤退はあり得ない。会長、社長も覚悟を決めてくれ。６０歳以上が現地へ行けばいい。自分はその覚悟でやる。撤退はあり得ない。撤退したら、東電は必ずつぶれる。」

これは同行した官邸の若いスタッフの聞き取りのメモを起こしたものです。

2号機の損傷

私が東電本店で、撤退しないでぎりぎりまで頑張ってほしいと強く要請した直後の３月１５日午前６時頃、２号機原子炉の圧力抑制室（サプレッションチャンバー）付近で大きな衝撃音が発生したとの報告を現地対策本部から入りました。同時に格納容器内の圧力が大気圧と同じになりました。サプレッションチャンバーの一部に穴が開いたものとみられます。その後の検証では、放射性物質の流出が一番多かったのが2号機でした。格納容器全体が破壊していれば、最悪シナリオ通りの展開になっていた可能性が高いのです。また格納容器内の圧力が下がったことにより、2号機への注水が可能となりました。

反転攻勢

東電本店に政府・東電統合対策本部を設置してからは情報の流れが格段に良くなりました。使用済み燃料プールへの放水作業でも自衛隊や警察との協力体制が大きく改善されました。

菅　直人

　放射能に一方的に攻め込まれた原発事故に対して、反転攻勢の動きが始まったのは、統合対策本部が立ち上がった翌日、自衛隊が使用済み燃料プールへの注水のためにヘリを飛ばした３月１６日からでした。１６日は原発上空の放射線量が高かったため、ヘリからの注水を見送りましたが、１７日は決死の覚悟で注水を実施しました。これを契機に、自衛隊をはじめ消防、警察など、日本を救うため命懸けで頑張ろうと士気が高まりました。さらに1，2，3号の格納容器内の圧力が低下したことで、注水が可能となりました。その結果、核燃料を冷却ができるようになり、温度が徐々に下がり、各原発は安定化に向かいました。

神の御加護

もし、ベントが遅れた格納容器が圧力の上昇で、ゴム風船が割れるように全体が崩壊する爆発を起こしていたら、最悪のシナリオは避けられませんでした。しかし幸いに、格納容器は全体としては崩壊せず、部分的な損傷で済んだので、最悪のシナリオは免れました。

　この様に最悪のシナリオを免れることができたのは、現場で最後まで頑張りぬいてくれた東電関係者、自衛隊員、消防隊員、警察官の本当に命を懸けた努力のおかげです。しかしそれだけではありません。私は「神のご加護」があったおかげだと感じています。最悪に事態が回避されたのにはいくつかの幸運な偶然が重なりました。４号機の使用済み核燃料プールに水があったこともその一つです。工事の遅れで事故当時、４号機の原子炉上部は水で満たされており、プールとの間の仕切り版がたわんで、原発上部の水が使用済み燃料のプールに流れ込んだとされています。もしプールの水がなくなっていれば、プール内に移されていた使用中の核燃料がメルトダウンし、最悪のシナリオは避けられませんでした。まさに神の御加護があったのです。

　こうして「最悪のシナリオ」は幸運にも遠ざかり、具体的な避難計画の立案を指示するという事態にまでは至らず、「5千万人避難のシミュレーション」は私の頭の中に留まりました。しかし、現在に至るまで、私の脳裏には常に5千万人の避難という「最悪のシナリオ」は居座り続けています。

事故の原因

福島原発事故が起きた原因はどこにあったのでしょうか。直接の原因は東日本大震災の地震と津波で福島第一原発の全電源が喪失したからです。しかし、もともと日本は地震が多く、福島原発のある海岸は歴史上何度も津波に襲われています。そうしたことを十分考慮しないで原発を建設したために発生した事故です。

　福島第一原発のサイトが建設された場所はもともと海岸に面した標高35メートルの高台でした。それをわざわざ海面から10メートルの高さまで土を削って、こうして低くしたところに原子炉を建設したからです。35メートルの高台であれば、津波は到達せず、事故は起きていません。海水を冷却に使うのにポンプに要する電力代を安くするため、低くしたといわれています。また事故の起こる数年前には東電内で17メートルの津波の可能性を検討しましたが、そのための対策を打たなかったために事故を招いたといわれています。現在裁判で責任が争われています。

エネルギー計画を白紙に戻す

日本では福島原発事故前には電力の約３０％を原発で賄っており、2030年までには原発の比率を50％まで上げる計画でした。私は福島原発事故の後、原発比率を50％まで上げるという従来のエネルギー基本計画を白紙に戻し、脱原発に方向転換を図りました。更に大地震の震源地となる可能性が高いとされる浜岡原発の稼働を止めるように中部電力に要請し、受け入れさせました。

　そして原発に代わり、再生可能エネルギーによる発電を拡大させるために、20年前にドイツで導入された固定価格買い取り制度を導入しました。そして私が2011年9月に総理を辞任した後に、同じ民主党の野田氏が総理に就任し、2030年代に原発をゼロにすることを決めました。

　しかし残念ながら2012年の総選挙で民主党は大敗し、自民党が政権に返り咲きました。自民党は原発の発電量を20〜22%として維持することを決めました。そして現在残っている44基の原発を順次再稼働させようとしています。しかし国民の多くは原発の再稼働に

反対しており、裁判所が停止を命ずる例もあり、現在稼働している原発は全国で3基にとどまっています。

福島原発の現状

福島原発事故は今も収束していません。放射能汚染のため今でも10万人以上の人が避難しています。原子炉のうち1，2，3号機がメルトダウンし、現在も冷却のために燃料デブリに注水を続けていますが、注入した水の一部は格納容器から汚染水となって漏れ出ています。東電や経産省はスリーマイルの事故の例を参考に、４０年程度の期間で、デブリを取り出し、廃炉作業を完了する計画を立てています。しかし私はまず不可能だとみています。スリーマイル事故では圧力容器は健全で、デブリも圧力容器内にとどまっていました。そのため、スリーマイル原発の廃炉作業では冠水法つまり圧力容器を水で満たす方法で、放射線を遮断してデブリの取り出し作業ができました。しかし、福島原発の１，２，３号機はいずれも圧力容器の底が熱で溶けて大きな穴が開いています。そのため、デブリは格納容器内に散乱しています。格納容器内の放射線量は1分で致死量に達する極めて高いレベルにあります。そして水を張るには格納容器全体に水を入れる必要がありますが、格納容器自体が損傷しており、スリーマイルの例のように冠水法をとることは極めてむつかしいのです。

　チェルノブイリ事故では３０年経過して、石棺から漏れる放射能を遮断するために巨大な金属製のドームで４号機を覆いました。しかし、デブリの取り出しは全くめどが立っていません。福島原発も廃炉には100年以上の年月がかかると私は見ています。

省エネと再生可能エネルギー

日本では福島原発事故をきっかけにエネルギーへの国民的関心が高まり、エネルギー消費の状況が大きく変わってきています。原発事故以前の2010年に比べて今日、エネルギー消費は10%以上減少しました。これは国民の省エネ意識が高まり、生産現場でもビルや住宅でも省エネに向けた改革が進んだ結果です。

　住宅についても窓ガラスを二重、三重にするなど省エネ住宅が拡大しており、屋根に太陽光パネルを設置して光熱費がゼロの住宅も多くなっています。私の家も2013年に省エネ住宅に建て替え、屋根に5キロワットの太陽光パネルを設置した結果、エネルギー消費はマイナスとなり、光熱費もほぼゼロとなっています。

FITと導入で再生可能エネルギーが拡大

福島原発事故以前、多くの国で風力や太陽光発電が拡大していたにもかかわらず、日本では水力発電が電力の約10％を占めるだけで、それ以外の再エネの活用は進んでいませんでした。その理由は原発を推進する勢力の力が強く、再エネを抑圧してきたからです。
　私は脱原発、脱化石燃料を実現するためには太陽光、風力、バイオマスなど再エネによる発電を促進する必要があると考えました。そしてドイツで20年前から実施されている固定価格買い取り制度（FIT）が必要と考え、福島原発事故の3か月後、固定価格買い取り制度法案を、私の総理としての最後の仕事として成立させました。FIT制度の導入後、日本では太陽光発電を中心に再エネが大きく伸びています。全国各地に太陽光発電所が建設され、発電量は2015年までに4万5000GWhで原発5基分に達し、2020年までには原発10基分を超える発電量となる見込みです。

農林業と再エネ電力供給業との兼業

近年日本では、農業と太陽光発電の兼業の可能性が注目されています。日本の平野部には広い水田が広がっています。しかし、近年コメの値段が大きく下がり、水田の稲作では十分な収入が得られず、農業人口は減り続けています。最近、水田による稲作や野菜栽培の畑作と同時に太陽光発電を兼業で行う方法が開発され、注目を集めています。具体的には、水田や畑に高さ3メートル程度の柱を立て、間隔をあけてソーラーパネルを設置するソーラーシェアリングと呼ばれる方式です。この方式では太陽光の一部は作物に、一部は太陽光パネルにシェアされます。日照時間の長い日本ではこの方式

で十分稲や野菜が育ち、同時に太陽光発電も行えます。日本の農地面積は４６０万ｈａあり、この方式は広がれば日本が必要とする電力の大半を農地から供給できます。

諸外国の原発事情

最後に私が招かれた国々の原発事情について紹介します。ドイツは福島原発から数か月後に2022年原発ゼロを決定しました。本来ならば日本こそどの国よりも早く原発ゼロを決めるべきだと思っていますが、残念ながらそうはなっていません。

　福島原発事故後最初に招かれたのは、アメリカのカリフォルニア州のサンオノフレ原発の再稼働に反対していた市民グループでした。福島原発事故当時アメリカのＮＲＣの委員長であったヤツコさん達と現地でシンポジウムを行いました。その数日後、サンオノフレ原発を所有するエジソン社は廃炉を決定しました。アメリカでは地震の多い西海岸には原発は少なく、地震の少ない東海岸におおく立地しています。アメリカでも原発の新設以上に廃炉が進んでおり、現在アメリカの原発は100基を切っています。

　その後韓国、ポーランド、イギリス、台湾などの反対運動からも招かれました。台湾では新設した第4原発を稼働させず、2025年には原発ゼロとすることを決めました。アメリカに並ぶ原発大国フランスでも、オランド大統領は電力供給の原発比率を75％から50％に下げることを公約し、増設を抑制しています。

　原発の建設が減少し始めた最大の理由はコストが上がり、再エネ電力より原発による電力料金の方が高くなり、採算が取れなくなってきたことです。たとえばイギリスでは政府は古い原発を廃炉にし、新たな原発を建設することを認めていますが、民間からの資金が集まらず、政府に支援を求めています。

全ての国でエネルギー自給が可能

エネルギー専門家によれば、太陽が地球に降り注ぐエネルギーの量は人類が使っているエネルギーの一万倍と言われています。つま

り、太陽エネルギーの一万分の一を電力や熱として有効に使えば、人類が必要とするエネルギーは充足できる理屈です。そして、今日の技術を活用すれば地球上のほとんどの国は、自国の太陽光や風力など再生可能エネルギーを活用すれば必要なエネルギーを自給できるはずです。

　すべての国が自国で必要とするエネルギーを自給できるようになれば、石油の争奪戦のようなエネルギーをめぐる国際紛争もなくなります。

　この様に脱原発、脱化石燃料を実現し、再生可能な自然エネルギーを活用することで平和な世界を実現する道も開けます。私はこれからもそうした目標に向かって頑張ってゆきたいと考えています。

著者プロフィール

菅直人（1946年10月10日生まれ）は、2010年6月から2011年9月まで内閣総理大臣を務めた。また、菅は、副総理、財務大臣、厚生大臣、国家戦略担当大臣などを歴任した。

山口県のサラリーマンの息子として育った菅は、東京工業大学で物理学を学び、卒業後、特許事務所に勤務。

3回の落選を経て、1980年、小党であった社会民主連合から衆議院選挙に出馬して、当選。1990年代半ばには、自由民主党との連立内閣に厚生大臣として入閣。HIVウィルスに汚染された血液製剤をめぐるスキャンダルを暴き出して一躍有名となる。

その後、民主党の結党に参画しをリードし、2009年9月の選挙で自由民主党を倒し、政権交代に貢献した。民主党から内閣総理大臣となった鳩山由紀夫が辞職後、2010年に菅は内閣総理大臣となる。しかし、ねじれ国会、停滞する経済、そして肥大化する国家債務を引き継ぎ、震災福島原発事故の後6ヶ月で辞任に追い込まれることになった。

エイナウディ・センターについて

マリオ・エイナウディ国際学センターは、1961年、コーネル大学における世界の諸地域、諸国家、諸文化、諸言語について研究と教育を強化することを目的として設立された。1990年、センターの創立者で、政治学者であったマリオ・エイナウディの名が冠された。今日、センターには、特定地域の研究や特定テーマの研究をする数々のプログラムがある。また、講演シリーズ、学術会議などのイベントを組織するほか、教官及び学生に研究助成などの支援を提供し、様々な分野の研究者を集めて、複雑な国際問題に取り組んでいる。

Milton Keynes UK
Ingram Content Group UK Ltd.
UKHW011030060724
445093UK00005B/134

9 781501 726934